# Specimen Aural Tests

from 2011

with 2 CDs

## Grades 1–3

ABRSM

# Introduction

Minor modifications to some aural tests took effect for ABRSM Practical graded music exams from January 2011 (all subjects except Jazz). For further details of the changes visit www.abrsm.org/aural. This book of specimen tests provides practice examples which demonstrate the style and difficulty level of the tests at Grades 1 to 3.

Listening lies at the heart of all good music-making. Developing aural awareness is fundamental to musical training because having a 'musical ear' impacts on all aspects of musicianship. By integrating aural activities in imaginative ways throughout the lesson, preparation for the aural tests within an exam will be a natural extension of what is already an essential part of the learning experience.

## Using the specimen tests

When preparing for an exam, these specimen tests will provide valuable practice material to help prepare candidates for what to expect on the day. Guided by the examples provided, teachers will also be able to devise their own exercises, ideally using music their students are currently working on.

## What does each test involve?

A description of the tasks involved in each test, as well as any relevant parameters, is given in the left-hand column at the start of each set of tests. The same information can also be found in the syllabus booklet.

## What will happen in the exam?

The examiner will deliver each test following a set of spoken words and instructions (referred to as the 'rubric'). All music extracts will be played on the piano, and the examiner will be ready to prompt the candidate if necessary where there is hesitation. In this book, the examiner rubric is printed in the right-hand column at the start of each set of tests and at the top of any subsequent pages, so that teachers are able to deliver the tests to their students in a way that mirrors the exam experience.

For any test that requires a sung response, it is pitch rather than vocal quality that is being assessed. The examiner will be happy to adapt to the vocal range of the candidate, whose responses may be sung to any vowel (or consonant followed by vowel), or hummed or whistled (and at a different octave, if appropriate).

Where tests require a spoken response, candidates are encouraged to use Italian terms where appropriate, but there will be no disadvantage to those who do not, provided that their response is equally clear and accurate.

## Using the CDs

The CDs include recordings of all the tests in this book, along with the spoken rubric. Answers are given for all tests that require a spoken response. An answer space is provided on the CD, but if extra thinking time is required simply pause the recording. Track numbers are printed at the start of each music example, and there is also a track list at the back of the book.

## Mock tests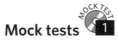

On the CDs, at the end of each grade, there is a set of tests presented in order, as they would be in the exam, to form a mock test. The relevant tests are marked in the book with the symbol shown above. The mock tests are also available as free downloads from www.abrsm.org/mockauraltests.

## Answers

Model answers for Tests 1D, 2C, 2D, 3C and 3D are printed at the back of this book, as a guide to the sort of responses that would be successful in the exam. Answers are also given on the CDs for any parts of the tests that require a spoken response. In some cases there are other ways of responding that would be equally successful, so the answers should be used only as a guide. It should also be noted that in an exam the examiner will not provide answers.

## How are the aural tests marked?

The mark for aural tests is arrived at by making an overall assessment of the candidate's aural skills, knowledge and understanding during the set of tests as a whole, and relating this to the assessment criteria shown below. Rather than starting at zero and awarding marks as the tests proceed, or at 18 and then deducting marks, examiners use the principle of marking positively or negatively from the pass mark. The mark then reflects the cumulative balance of strengths and weaknesses that the candidate has demonstrated, taking into account the accuracy, perceptiveness and quality of the responses given.

## Assessment criteria (all grades)

| | |
|---|---|
| **Distinction** **17–18** | • Accurate throughout<br>• Musically perceptive<br>• Confident response |
| **Merit** **15–16** | • Strengths significantly outweigh weaknesses<br>• Musically aware<br>• Secure response |
| **Pass** **12–14** | • Strengths just outweigh weaknesses<br>• Cautious response |
| **Below Pass** **9–11** | • Weaknesses outweigh strengths<br>• Uncertain response |
| **6–8** | • Inaccuracy throughout<br>• Vague response |
| **0** | • No work offered |

## Access (for candidates with specific needs)

Deaf or hearing-impaired candidates may opt to respond to alternative tests in place of the standard tests, if requested at the time of entry. The syllabus for these tests is available free on request from ABRSM. For further information about alternative tests and access for candidates with specific needs please contact ABRSM's Access Co-ordinator or visit the website.

Telephone +44 (0)20 7636 5400
Textphone +44 (0)20 7637 2582
Email accesscoordinator@abrsm.ac.uk
www.abrsm.org/specialneeds

## Other aural training resources from ABRSM

For further examples and comprehensive advice on preparing candidates for aural tests, teachers are referred to the new edition of *Aural Training in Practice* (2011).

Please note that the music extracts in this book have been freely adapted where necessary for the purpose of the aural tests.

First published in 2010 by ABRSM (Publishing) Ltd, a wholly owned subsidiary of ABRSM, 24 Portland Place, London W1B 1LU, United Kingdom

Reprinted in 2010, 2011, 2014

© 2010 by The Associated Board of the Royal Schools of Music

Cover and text design by Vermillion
Music and text origination by Andrew Jones
Additional text setting by Hope Services Ltd
Printed in England by Halstan & Co. Ltd, Amersham, Bucks.

## 1A Grade 1

**To clap the pulse of a piece played by the examiner, and to identify whether it is in two time or three time.** The examiner will start playing the passage, and the candidate should join in as soon as possible, clapping in time and giving a louder clap on the strong beats. The examiner will then ask whether the music is in two time or three time. The candidate is *not* required to state the time signature.

*First, clap in time while I play. Join in as soon as you can and give a louder clap on the strong beats.*

[Play the entire piece.]

*Is it in two time or three time? ... Thank you.*

6 **Ritmico** — Country dance

7 **Moderato** — Le Couppey

8 **Allegretto comodo** — Kirnberger

9 **Moderato** — Pleyel

37 **Lively** — Folk tune

**To sing as 'echoes' three phrases played by the examiner.** The phrases will be two bars long, in a major key, and within the range of tonic–mediant. First the examiner will play the key-chord and the starting note (the tonic) and then count in two bars. After the examiner has played each phrase, the candidate should sing back the echo without a pause, keeping in time.

*Next I'd like you to sing three phrases as echoes. Here is the key-chord* [play] *and your starting note* [play].

[Count in two bars.] *... Thank you.*

AB 3575

**To identify where a change in pitch occurs during a phrase played by the examiner.** The phrase will be two bars long, in a major key, and the change will affect only one of the notes. First the examiner will play the key-chord and the tonic and then count in two bars. The examiner will play the phrase twice, making the change in the second playing, after which the candidate should state whether the change was near the beginning or near the end. If necessary, the examiner will play both versions of the phrase again (although this will affect the assessment).

*Now I'll play a phrase twice, but with a change to one of the notes the second time. Tell me whether the change was near the beginning or near the end. Here is the key-chord* [play] *and the tonic* [play]*.* [Count in two bars and play the phrase for the first time.] *And now with the change.* [Play the altered phrase without counting in.] *Was the change near the beginning or near the end? … Thank you.*

*Now I'll play a phrase twice, but with a change to one of the notes the second time. Tell me whether the change was near the beginning or near the end. Here is the key-chord* [play] *and the tonic* [play]. [Count in two bars and play the phrase for the first time.] *And now with the change.* [Play the altered phrase without counting in.] *Was the change near the beginning or near the end? ... Thank you.*

**6**

beginning / end

**7**

beginning / end

**8**

beginning / end

**9**

beginning / end

**10**

beginning / end

AB 3575

**To answer questions about two features of a piece played by the examiner.** Before playing, the examiner will tell the candidate which two features the questions will be about. The first will be dynamics (loud/quiet, or sudden/gradual changes); the second will be articulation (smooth/detached).

*Listen to this piece, then I'll ask you about loud or quiet playing and about smooth or detached notes.*

[After playing, ask one question at a time: dynamics (either 'loud/quiet' or 'changes'), and then articulation.] **...**

*Thank you.*

Dynamics (loud/quiet): *The music began loudly; did it stay loud all the way through?*
        (changes): *Did the changes from loud to quiet playing happen suddenly or gradually?*
Articulation: *Were the quieter phrases played with smooth or detached notes?*

Dynamics (loud/quiet): *Where was the quietest part of the music?*
        (changes): *Was the change from quiet to loud playing sudden or gradual?*
Articulation: *At the beginning, were the notes smooth or detached?*

*Listen to this piece, then I'll ask you about loud or
quiet playing and about smooth or detached notes.*

[After playing, ask one question at a time:
dynamics (either 'loud/quiet' or 'changes'), and
then articulation.] **...**

*Thank you.*

Alan Richardson

Dynamics (loud/quiet): *The music began quite loudly; did it stay the same all the way through?*
(changes): *Were the changes in loud and quiet playing sudden or gradual?*
Articulation: *Were the notes smooth or detached?*

Dynamics (loud/quiet): *Where was the quietest part of the music?*
(changes): *Was the change from quiet in the middle to loud at the end made suddenly or gradually?*
Articulation: *At the beginning, were the notes smooth or detached?*

Le Couppey

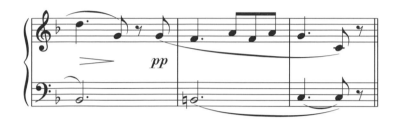

Dynamics (loud/quiet): ***Where was the loudest part of the music? And the quietest?***
      (changes): ***Did the change from loud to quiet playing happen suddenly or gradually?***
Articulation: ***At the start, were the notes played smoothly or were they detached?***

Grieg

Dynamics (loud/quiet): ***Where was the loudest part of the music?***
      (changes): ***Did the change from loud to quiet playing happen suddenly or gradually?***
Articulation: ***At the beginning, were the notes smooth or detached?***

*Listen to this piece, then I'll ask you about loud or
quiet playing and about smooth or detached notes.*

[After playing, ask one question at a time:
dynamics (either 'loud/quiet' or 'changes'), and
then articulation.] ...

*Thank you.*

Dynamics (loud/quiet): ***Which was quieter – the beginning or the end?***
      (changes): ***Was the change from quiet to loud playing made suddenly or gradually?***
Articulation: ***Was the playing mainly smooth or detached?***

Dynamics (loud/quiet): ***Which was louder – the beginning or the end?***
      (changes): ***When the music became loud towards the end, was this a sudden or a gradual change?***
Articulation: ***When the music was quiet at the beginning, were the notes smooth or detached?***

Allegretto

Gossec

Dynamics (loud/quiet): *Where was the loudest part of the music?*

(changes): *Towards the end, did the music become quiet suddenly or gradually?*

Articulation: *At the beginning, were the notes smooth or detached?*

Con brio

Verdi

Dynamics (loud/quiet): *The music began loudly; did it stay the same all the way through?*

(changes): *Did the music become quieter suddenly or gradually?*

Articulation: *At the start, were the notes smooth or detached?*

## 2A Grade 2

**To clap the pulse of a piece played by the examiner, and to identify whether it is in two time or three time.** The examiner will start playing the passage, and the candidate should join in as soon as possible, clapping in time and giving a louder clap on the strong beats. The examiner will then ask whether the music is in two time or three time. The candidate is *not* required to state the time signature.

*First, clap in time while I play. Join in as soon as you can and give a louder clap on the strong beats.*

[Play the entire piece.]

*Is it in two time or three time? ... Thank you.*

45 **Andante** — Bononcini

46 **Moderato** — Coleridge-Taylor

47 **Allegro moderato** — Mayer

*First, clap in time while I play. Join in as soon as you can and give a louder clap on the strong beats.*

[Play the entire piece.]

*Is it in two time or three time? ... Thank you.*

**To sing as 'echoes' three phrases played by the examiner.** The phrases will be two bars long, in a major key, and within the range of tonic–dominant. First the examiner will play the key-chord and the starting note (the tonic) and then count in two bars. After the examiner has played each phrase, the candidate should sing back the echo without a pause, keeping in time.

*Next I'd like you to sing three phrases as echoes. Here is the key-chord* [play] *and your starting note* [play].

[Count in two bars.] *... Thank you.*

1

2

3

4

5

*Next I'd like you to sing three phrases as echoes.*
*Here is the key-chord* [play] *and your starting*
*note* [play].

[Count in two bars.] *... Thank you.*

**To identify a change in either pitch or rhythm during a phrase played by the examiner.** The phrase will be two bars long, in a major key. First the examiner will play the key-chord and the tonic and then count in two bars. The examiner will play the phrase twice, making the change in the second playing, after which the candidate should identify the change by describing it, or singing/clapping. If necessary, the examiner will play both versions of the phrase again (although this will affect the assessment).

*Now I'll play a phrase twice, but with a change in either pitch or rhythm the second time. Tell me what the difference was. Here is the key-chord [play] and the tonic [play]. [Count in two bars and play the phrase for the first time.] And now with the change. [Play the altered phrase without counting in.] How was it different? ... Thank you.*

1.

pitch

rhythm

2.

© Copyright 1950 by Boosey & Co.
Reproduced by permission of Boosey & Hawkes
Music Publishers Ltd

pitch

rhythm

3.

pitch

rhythm

*Now I'll play a phrase twice, but with a change in either pitch or rhythm the second time. Tell me what the difference was. Here is the key-chord* [play] *and the tonic* [play]. [Count in two bars and play the phrase for the first time.] **And now with the change.** [Play the altered phrase without counting in.] *How was it different? … Thank you.*

Allegro — Donizetti

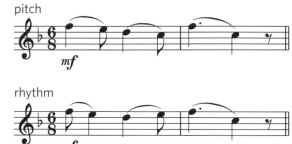

pitch

rhythm

Andante con moto — Schubert

pitch

rhythm

Moderato — Sullivan

pitch

rhythm

**To answer questions about two features of a piece played by the examiner.** Before playing, the examiner will tell the candidate which two features the questions will be about. The first will be *one* of the following: dynamics (loud/quiet, or sudden/gradual changes), articulation (smooth/detached); the second will be tempo (becoming slower/faster, or staying the same).

*Listen to this piece, then I'll ask you about ...*
[choose one of the following: *loud or quiet playing, smooth or detached notes*] *and about tempo change.*

[After playing, ask one question at a time.]* ...

***Thank you.***

Purcell

Dynamics (loud/quiet): ***Where was the quietest part of the music?***

   (changes): ***Did the change from quiet to loud playing happen suddenly or gradually?***

Articulation: ***At the beginning, were the notes smooth or detached?***

Tempo: ***Was there any change in the speed of the music, or did it always stay the same?***

Heller

Dynamics (loud/quiet): ***Where was the loudest part of the music?***

   (changes): ***Did the change to quiet playing at the end happen suddenly or gradually?***

Articulation: ***Was the playing mainly smooth or detached?***

Tempo: ***Did the speed of the music change at all, or did it stay the same throughout?***

* If 'loud or quiet playing' is selected, ask either the question marked 'loud/quiet' or the question marked 'changes', but not both.

***Listen to this piece, then I'll ask you about ...***
[choose one of the following: *loud or quiet playing,
smooth or detached notes*] ***and about tempo change.***

[After playing, ask one question at a time.]* **...**

***Thank you.***

Dynamics (loud/quiet): ***Where was the loudest part of the music?***
       (changes): ***Did the change from quiet to loud playing near the beginning happen suddenly or gradually?***
Articulation: ***Was the beginning played with smooth or detached notes?***
Tempo: ***Was there any change in the speed of the music, or did it stay the same throughout?***

Dynamics (loud/quiet): ***Where was the loudest part of the music? And the quietest?***
       (changes): ***Did the changes in loud and quiet playing happen suddenly or gradually?***
Articulation: ***Did the music have mainly smooth or detached notes?***
Tempo: ***Was there any change in the speed of the music, or did it always stay the same?***

* If 'loud or quiet playing' is selected, ask either the question(s) marked 'loud/quiet' or the question marked 'changes', but not both.

Heller

Dynamics (loud/quiet): **Where was the quietest part of the music?**

       (changes): **Did the changes in loud and quiet playing happen suddenly or gradually?**

Articulation: **Was the playing mainly smooth or detached?**

Tempo: **Was there any change in the speed of the music, or did it always stay the same?**

Jeremiah Clarke

Dynamics (loud/quiet): **Where was the loudest part of the music?**

       (changes): **Was the change from quiet to loud playing near the end sudden or gradual?**

Articulation: **At the beginning, was the melody played with smooth or detached notes?**

Tempo: **Did the speed of the music change anywhere, or did it always stay the same?**

***Listen to this piece, then I'll ask you about ...***
[choose one of the following: *loud or quiet playing,
smooth or detached notes*] **and about tempo change.**

[After playing, ask one question at a time.]* **...**

***Thank you.***

Dynamics (loud/quiet): ***Where was the loudest part of the music?***
       (changes): ***Did the changes in loud and quiet playing happen suddenly or gradually?***
Articulation: ***Were the notes played mainly smoothly, or were they detached?***
Tempo: ***Was there any change in the speed of the music, or did it always stay the same?***

Dynamics (loud/quiet): ***Where was the loudest part of the music?***
       (changes): ***Did the change from loud to quiet playing happen suddenly or gradually?***
Articulation: ***Was the playing mainly smooth or detached?***
Tempo: ***Did the speed of the music change at all, or did it stay the same throughout?***

* If 'loud or quiet playing' is selected, ask either the question(s) marked 'loud/quiet' or the question marked 'changes', but not both.

Moderato (Tempo di Polka) — Tchaikovsky

Dynamics (loud/quiet): *Where was the loudest part of the music?*

(changes): *Were the changes in loud and quiet playing sudden or gradual?*

Articulation: *Were the notes mainly smooth or detached?*

Tempo: *Was there any change in the speed of the music, or did it always stay the same?*

Andante — Liszt

Dynamics (loud/quiet): *Where was the loudest part of the music? And the quietest?*

(changes): *Were the changes in loud and quiet playing sudden or gradual?*

Articulation: *Were the notes mostly smooth or detached?*

Tempo: *Was there any change in the speed of the music, or did it always stay the same?*

To clap the pulse of a piece played by the examiner, **and to identify whether it is in two time, three time or four time.** The examiner will start playing the passage, and the candidate should join in as soon as possible, clapping in time and giving a louder clap on the strong beats. The examiner will then ask whether the music is in two time, three time or four time. The candidate is *not* required to state the time signature.

*First, clap in time while I play. Join in as soon as you can and give a louder clap on the strong beats.*

[Play the entire piece.]

*Is it in two time, three time or four time? ...*

*Thank you.*

Reproduced from 'Holiday Pictures' published by Stainer & Bell Ltd
23 Gruneisen Road, London N3 1DZ, England www.stainer.co.uk

AB 3575

*First, clap in time while I play. Join in as soon as you can and give a louder clap on the strong beats.*

[Play the entire piece.]

*Is it in two time, three time or four time? ...*

*Thank you.*

Mozart

Karganov

Bryan Kelly

**To sing as 'echoes' three phrases played by the examiner.** The phrases will be two bars long, in a major or minor key, and within the range of an octave. First the examiner will play the key-chord and the starting note and then count in two bars. After the examiner has played each phrase, the candidate should sing back the echo without a pause, keeping in time.

*Next I'd like you to sing three phrases as echoes. Here is the key-chord* [play] *and your starting note* [play].

[Count in two bars.] *... Thank you.*

*Next I'd like you to sing three phrases as echoes.*
*Here is the key-chord* [play] *and your starting*
*note* [play].

[Count in two bars.] *... Thank you.*

**To identify a change in either pitch or rhythm during a phrase played by the examiner.** The phrase will be up to four bars long, in a major or minor key. First the examiner will play the key-chord and the tonic and then count in two bars. The examiner will play the phrase twice, making the change in the second playing, after which the candidate should identify the change by describing it, or singing/clapping.
If necessary, the examiner will play both versions of the phrase again (although this will affect the assessment).

*Now I'll play a phrase twice, but with a change in either pitch or rhythm the second time. Tell me what the difference was. Here is the key-chord* [play] *and the tonic* [play]. [Count in two bars and play the phrase for the first time.] *And now with the change.* [Play the altered phrase without counting in.] *How was it different? ... Thank you.*

*Now I'll play a phrase twice, but with a change in either pitch or rhythm the second time. Tell me what the difference was. Here is the key-chord* [play] *and the tonic* [play]. [Count in two bars and play the phrase for the first time.] *And now with the change.* [Play the altered phrase without counting in.] *How was it different? ... Thank you.*

4

pitch

5

pitch

6

pitch

**To answer questions about two features of a piece played by the examiner.** Before playing, the examiner will tell the candidate which two features the questions will be about. The first will be *one* of the following: dynamics (loud/quiet, or sudden/gradual changes), articulation (smooth/detached), tempo (becoming slower/faster, or staying the same); the second will be tonality (major/minor key).

*Listen to this piece, then I'll ask you about ...*
[choose one of the following: *loud or quiet playing, smooth or detached notes, tempo change*] *and about major or minor key.*

[After playing, ask one question at a time.]* ...

*Thank you.*

Dynamics (loud/quiet): *Of the three sections in the music, which one was the loudest?*
   (changes): *Did the change from quiet to loud playing happen suddenly or gradually?*
Articulation: *Was the upper part played with mainly smooth or detached notes?*
Tempo: *Was there any change in the speed of the music, or did it always stay the same?*
Tonality: *Did the piece end in a major key or in a minor key?*

Dynamics (loud/quiet): *Where was the quietest point in the music?*
   (changes): *Were the changes in loud and quiet playing sudden or gradual?*
Articulation: *Was the piece played in a smooth or detached style?*
Tempo: *Did the speed of the music change at all, or did it always stay the same?*
Tonality: *Was the piece in a major key or in a minor key?*

* If 'loud or quiet playing' is selected, ask either the question marked 'loud/quiet' or the question marked 'changes', but not both.

*Listen to this piece, then I'll ask you about ...*
[choose one of the following: *loud or quiet playing,
smooth or detached notes, tempo change*] *and about
major or minor key.*

[*After playing, ask one question at a time.*]* **...**

*Thank you.*

Dynamics (loud/quiet): ***Where was the quietest part of the music?***
          (changes): ***Were the changes in loud and quiet playing sudden or gradual?***
Articulation: ***Was the quiet phrase played with smooth or detached notes?***
Tempo: ***Did the speed of the music change, or did it always stay the same?***
Tonality: ***Was the piece in a major key or in a minor key?***

Dynamics (loud/quiet): ***Did the music begin loudly or quietly?***
          (changes): ***Was the loudest point in the music reached suddenly or gradually?***
Articulation: ***Was the ending smooth or detached?***
Tempo: ***Did the speed of the music change at all, or did it always stay the same?***
Tonality: ***Did the piece end in a major key or in a minor key?***

* If 'loud or quiet playing' is selected, ask either the question marked 'loud/quiet' or the question marked 'changes', but not both.

Dynamics (loud/quiet): ***Where was the loudest part of the music?***

(changes): ***Was the loudest point reached by a sudden or gradual change?***

Articulation: ***Was the melody played with mainly smooth or detached notes?***

Tempo: ***Was there any change in the speed of the music, or did it always stay the same?***

Tonality: ***Did the music end in a major key or in a minor key?***

Dynamics (loud/quiet): ***The music began loudly; did it stay loud throughout?***

(changes): ***Was the change from loud to quiet playing sudden or gradual?***

Articulation: ***Were the notes smooth or detached?***

Tempo: ***Was there any change in the speed of the music, or did it always stay the same?***

Tonality: ***Was the music in a major key or in a minor key?***

***Listen to this piece, then I'll ask you about ...***
[choose one of the following: *loud or quiet playing,
smooth or detached notes, tempo change*] ***and about
major or minor key.***

[After playing, ask one question at a time.]* **...**

***Thank you.***

Schumann

Dynamics (loud/quiet): ***Which was louder – the first half of the piece or the second half?***
       (changes): ***Was the change to very quiet playing made suddenly or gradually?***
Articulation: ***Was the playing smooth or detached?***
Tempo: ***Was there any change in the speed of the music, or did it always stay the same?***
Tonality: ***Was the piece in a major key or in a minor key?***

Grieg

Dynamics (loud/quiet): ***Where was the quietest point in the music?***
       (changes): ***Was the first change from quiet to loud playing sudden or gradual?***
Articulation: ***Were the quiet chords played with smooth or detached notes?***
Tempo: ***Was there any change in the speed of the music, or did it always stay the same?***
Tonality: ***Did the piece end in a major key or in a minor key?***

* If 'loud or quiet playing' is selected, ask either the question marked 'loud/quiet' or the question marked 'changes', but not both.

Kabalevsky

Dynamics (loud/quiet): ***Where was the loudest point in the music?***

     (changes): ***Did the change from quiet to loud playing happen suddenly or gradually?***

Articulation: ***Was the beginning played smoothly or was it detached?***

Tempo: ***Was there any change in the speed of the music, or did it always stay the same?***

Tonality: ***Did the piece end in a major key or in a minor key?***

*Listen to this piece, then I'll ask you about ...*
[choose one of the following: *loud or quiet playing,
smooth or detached notes, tempo change*] *and about
major or minor key.*

[After playing, ask one question at a time.]* **...**

*Thank you.*

Dynamics (loud/quiet): **Where was the quietest point in the piece?**
    (changes): **Was the change from quiet in the middle to loud at the end made suddenly or gradually?**
Articulation: **Were the notes smooth or detached?**
Tempo: **Was there any change in the speed of the music, or did it always stay the same?**
Tonality: **Was the piece in a major key or in a minor key?**

---

* If 'loud or quiet playing' is selected, ask either the question marked 'loud/quiet' or the question marked 'changes', but not both.

# Answers

Model answers for Tests 1D, 2C, 2D, 3C and 3D are printed here as a guide to the sort of responses that would be successful in an exam. Full credit would be given to these answers, if given promptly and confidently. However, they are neither definitive nor comprehensive and there are other ways of responding to the questions that would be equally successful. In Tests 2C and 3C there may be several different ways of correctly describing a change in rhythm (for Test 2C ex. 1, for example, 'The last note was longer' would also be correct); and instead of giving a spoken response, the candidate may clap or sing to show how the altered version was different.

Marks are not awarded for individual tests but reflect the candidate's overall performance during the set of tests as a whole. Candidates are encouraged to use Italian or other musical terms in their answers where appropriate. However, any clear description is acceptable, and in the answers below only English terms have been used. The assessment criteria are given on page 3.

## GRADE 1

### Test 1D

1. J. C. F. Bach
   Dynamics (loud/quiet): No
   (changes): Suddenly
   Articulation: Smooth

2. Haydn
   Dynamics (loud/quiet): In the middle
   (changes): Gradual
   Articulation: Detached

3. Alan Richardson
   Dynamics (loud/quiet): No
   (changes): Sudden
   Articulation: Smooth

4. Glinka
   Dynamics (loud/quiet): In the middle
   (changes): Gradually
   Articulation: Detached

5. Le Couppey
   Dynamics (loud/quiet): At the start; at the end
   (changes): Suddenly
   Articulation: Detached

6. Grieg
   Dynamics (loud/quiet): In the middle
   (changes): Gradually
   Articulation: Smooth

7. Hummel
   Dynamics (loud/quiet): The beginning
   (changes): Suddenly
   Articulation: Detached

8. Schubert
   Dynamics (loud/quiet): The end
   (changes): Gradual
   Articulation: Detached

9. Gossec
   Dynamics (loud/quiet): In the middle
   (changes): Gradually
   Articulation: Detached

10. Verdi
    Dynamics (loud/quiet): No
    (changes): Suddenly
    Articulation: Detached

39

# Answers

## GRADE 2

### Test 2C

1. **Haydn**
   Pitch: There was a lower note near the beginning
   Rhythm: There was a shorter note near the end

2. **Finzi**
   Pitch: There was a higher note near the beginning
   Rhythm: The first note was shorter

3. **Le Couppey**
   Pitch: There was a lower note near the beginning
   Rhythm: There was a dotted rhythm near the end

4. **Donizetti**
   Pitch: There was a lower note in the middle
   Rhythm: The first note was shorter

5. **Schubert**
   Pitch: There was a higher note in the middle
   Rhythm: There was a longer note near the end

6. **Sullivan**
   Pitch: There was a higher note near the end
   Rhythm: There was a dotted rhythm in the middle

### Test 2D

1. **Purcell**
   Dynamics (loud/quiet): In the middle
   (changes): Gradually
   Articulation: Detached
   Tempo: It stayed the same

2. **Heller**
   Dynamics (loud/quiet): Just before the end
   (changes): Suddenly
   Articulation: Smooth
   Tempo: It slowed down towards the end

3. **Schumann**
   Dynamics (loud/quiet): Just after the beginning
   (changes): Suddenly
   Articulation: Smooth
   Tempo: It got faster towards the end

4. **Fauré**
   Dynamics (loud/quiet): In the middle; at the end
   (changes): Gradually
   Articulation: Smooth
   Tempo: It slowed down towards the end

5. **Heller**
   Dynamics (loud/quiet): At the end
   (changes): Gradually
   Articulation: Smooth
   Tempo: It slowed down towards the end

6. **Jeremiah Clarke**
   Dynamics (loud/quiet): At the end
   (changes): Sudden
   Articulation: Detached
   Tempo: It stayed the same

7. **Schumann**
   Dynamics (loud/quiet): In the middle
   (changes): Gradually
   Articulation: Smoothly
   Tempo: It slowed down towards the end

8. **Handel**
   Dynamics (loud/quiet): At the beginning
   (changes): Suddenly
   Articulation: Smooth
   Tempo: It slowed down towards the end

9. **Tchaikovsky**
   Dynamics (loud/quiet): At the end
   (changes): Gradual
   Articulation: Detached
   Tempo: It stayed the same

10. **Liszt**
    Dynamics (loud/quiet): In the middle; at the end
    (changes): Gradual
    Articulation: Smooth
    Tempo: It slowed down towards the end

## GRADE 3

### Test 3C
1. Arcadelt
   Pitch: There was a lower note near the beginning
   Rhythm: There was a shorter note in the middle

2. Schumann
   Pitch: There was a lower note near the end
   Rhythm: There was a dotted rhythm near the beginning

3. Campra
   Pitch: There was a higher note near the end
   Rhythm: There were even notes near the beginning

4. Geminiani
   Pitch: There was a lower note near the end
   Rhythm: The second note was longer

5. Burgmüller
   Pitch: There was a lower note near the end
   Rhythm: There was a shorter note in the middle

6. Handel
   Pitch: There was a higher note in the middle
   Rhythm: There was a longer note near the end

### Test 3D
1. Hünten
   Dynamics (loud/quiet): The second section
   (changes): Suddenly
   Articulation: Detached
   Tempo: It slowed down in the middle
   Tonality: Major

2. Guilmant
   Dynamics (loud/quiet): At the end
   (changes): Gradual
   Articulation: Smooth
   Tempo: It stayed the same
   Tonality: Minor

3. Student song
   Dynamics (loud/quiet): The middle
   (changes): Sudden
   Articulation: Smooth
   Tempo: It stayed the same
   Tonality: Major

4. Volkmann
   Dynamics (loud/quiet): Loudly
   (changes): Gradually
   Articulation: Smooth
   Tempo: It slowed down near the end
   Tonality: Major

5. Chopin
   Dynamics (loud/quiet): In the second half/towards the end
   (changes): Gradual
   Articulation: Smooth
   Tempo: It slowed down towards the end
   Tonality: Minor

6. Purcell
   Dynamics (loud/quiet): No, the second half was quiet
   (changes): Sudden
   Articulation: Detached
   Tempo: It slowed down towards the end
   Tonality: Major

7. Schumann
   Dynamics (loud/quiet): The first half
   (changes): Gradually
   Articulation: Smooth
   Tempo: It slowed down towards the end
   Tonality: Major

8. Grieg
   Dynamics (loud/quiet): At the end
   (changes): Sudden
   Articulation: Detached
   Tempo: It slowed down towards the end
   Tonality: Minor

9. Kabalevsky
   Dynamics (loud/quiet): In the middle
   (changes): Gradually
   Articulation: Smoothly
   Tempo: It slowed down in the second half/near the end
   Tonality: Minor

10. Handel
    Dynamics (loud/quiet): In the middle
    (changes): Gradually
    Articulation: Detached
    Tempo: It stayed the same
    Tonality: Major

# CD track list

## GRADE 1

| Tracks | Test | Examples |
|---|---|---|
| 1–9 | 1A | 1–9 |
| 10–18 | 1B | 1–9 |
| 19–27 | 1C | 1–9 |
| 28–36 | 1D | 1–9 |
| 37–40 | Mock Test | |

## GRADE 2

| Tracks | Test | Examples |
|---|---|---|
| 41–49 | 2A | 1–9 |
| 50–58 | 2B | 1–9 |
| 59–63 | 2C | 1–5 |
| 64–72 | 2D | 1–9 |
| 73–76 | Mock Test | |

## GRADE 3

| Tracks | Test | Examples |
|---|---|---|
| 1–9 | 3A | 1–9 |
| 10–18 | 3B | 1–9 |
| 19–23 | 3C | 1–5 |
| 24–32 | 3D | 1–9 |
| 33–36 | Mock Test | |

Examiners: Juliet Barwell, Robin Zebaida

Recorded in Spring 2010 at Red Gables Studio, Greenford

Produced by Sebastian Forbes

Balance Engineering by Ken Blair

Audio Editing by Ken Blair

A BMP production for ABRSM Publishing

ABRSM (Publishing) Ltd is a wholly owned subsidiary of ABRSM